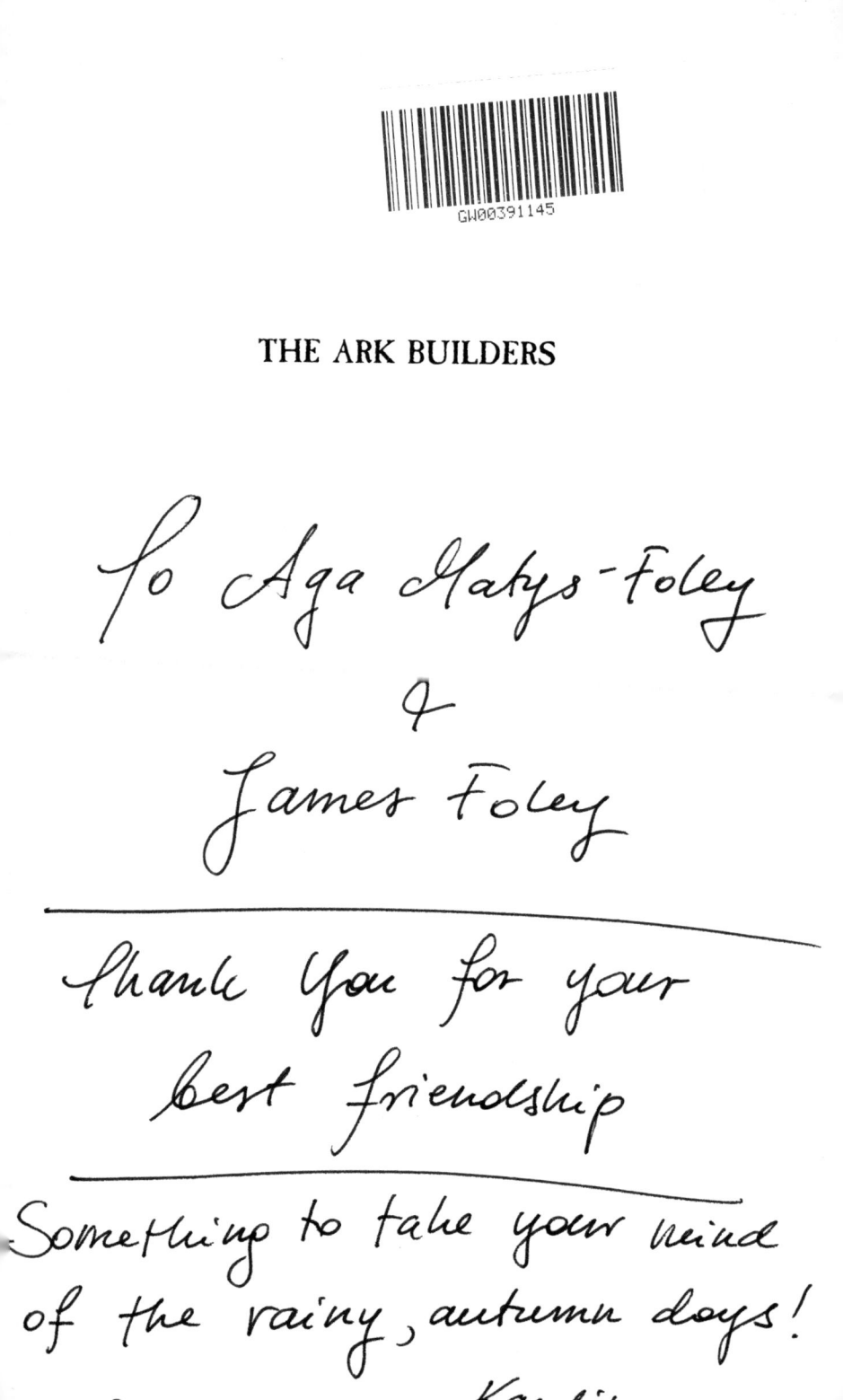

THE ARK BUILDERS

To Aga Matys-Foley
&
James Foley

Thank You for your
best friendship

Something to take your mind
of the rainy, autumn days!

.09. 18
Karolina

Also by Mary O'Donnell

Reading the Sunflowers in September (Salmon, 1990)
Spiderwoman's Third Avenue Rhapsody (Salmon, 1993)
Unlegendary Heroes (Salmon, 1998)
September Elegies (Lapwing, 2003)
The Place of Miracles (New Island, 2005)

THE ARK BUILDERS
Mary O'Donnell

To Karolina,
best wishes from
Mary o Donnell
8/3/12.

PUBLICATIONS
2009

Published by Arc Publications
Nanholme Mill, Shaw Wood Road
Todmorden OL14 6DA, UK
www.arcpublications.co.uk

978 1904614 58 6 pbk
978 1906570 04 0 hbk

ACKNOWLEDGEMENTS:
The author wishes to acknowledge the following journals
in which some of these poems first appeared: *Best New Irish
Poems 2008; Boletin Galega de Literatura (Galicia, Spain); Boyne
Berries; Cyphers; The Irish Times; Oxford Poetry;* the Irish pages of
*www.poetryinternational.org; Poetry Ireland Review; Revival (White
House Poets); The Salmon Anthology 2007; Southword; The Sting-
ing Fly* and *Stony Thursday*.
The poem 'Rain, That Thief' was winner of *The Flat Lake
Festival Poetry Award 2007*; 'Circus Haiku' was reproduced by
Barabbas Theatre Company for the Dublin Theatre Festival per-
formance of 'Circus', 2008; 'Seven Monaco Haiku' are pub-
lished by the *Princess Grace Irish Library, Monaco*; thanks also to
the Ireland Funds of Monaco for a residency at the Princess
Grace Irish Library during 2007.
Grateful acknowledgement is also made to Monaghan
County Council Arts Office for a Professional Artist's Bursary
in 2008 and to the Princess Grace Irish Library.

Cover painting: Bridget Flannery 'Textures of Time 2'
by kind permission of the artist.

Supported by
ARTS COUNCIL
ENGLAND

Editor for the UK and Ireland: John W. Clarke

To Maureen

Contents

I

History of Happen

It's the end of the world. Or a beginning.
What holds us back is etiquette of speech,

tricks and trades of dealing word for word.
When young, speech emerged in screams, the trees

wild with it, applause in clattering leaves
as we stomped down the fields wearing cloaks

of puce netting from a left-over bridesmaid's dress.
Tree language was natural, negative space

between the leaves, where the sky impressed itself
like hot wax, setting moments. *Clatter. Whisper.*

Whoosh. Shee. Hoo-ooo. Hawhhh...
The wind, skilled articulator, artful dancer

doing *pas de deux* with us alone,
ardent fans of the invisible and active.

Dialogue with Madam Alexei

And what does your psychiatrist
say about this?
I don't have one.
We're talking psychiatric illness here!
Don't you think it's time
to wake up, smell the coffee,
climb the tower, sing the line?
Yes-yes, time to do what's
necessary?

Or else? I'm a pro, all set
to pour the pills, flush the fluoxetine,
send seratonins up the Swannee,
doing the cha-cha
on how I've cheated everyone,
self above all?

Do you hear voices?
Only yours. You mean am I far edge
crazy?
No edge is needed.
There are Nobel Prize-winning
depressives! Besides,
you deserve to be happy.

Lady, you have no respect for effort.
I'm the complete survivor,
replete with trays of coloured pills
for ills we dare not speak of!

I hold history in place, blousefuls of greens,
reds, uppers, downers, sleepers, wakers,
all the time balancing the books, the rhyme,
the speech, the smile, and questions:
what carefully casual denims to wear,
how to suck pasta without making a mess,
to let my roots grow out or not?
Every night, I make it to bed,
not a mortuary slab, feel a pillow
beneath my head, not surgical knives
filleting my skull. A day of living
behind my own face has ended,
insanely sane, as much as you,
Madam Alexei, as much as you.

      Listen up! Here's an address.
No.
The night is dark,
and days are dark nights too.
God help, I admit to you,
God help me through
this wilderness of etiquette.
It's a killer.

Following Frida

That mono-brow wouldn't work today.
Girls wax the in-betweens, the ups and
downs, smooth, smooth. Sometimes,
the greenery around the hacienda
itches so much we sneeze and tickle,
create unnecessary frowns, a slippage.
There's always Dr. Death, of course,
his bright smile, that happy mouth
inviting us to pout and make kiss shapes.
Kiss, kiss! Kiss, kiss! he urges. His short needle
makes cushions of our worries. Little prick here,
another there, *there, there,*
it's all right darlings, growing old
needn't hurt so badly.
The hairs remind us, marching to link brow
to brow, shadowing our lips.
We want to be Frida, earnest with hair,
mocking Dr. Death's short needle
before it punctures our flesh.
Old, old! we shout the words he hates,
loose and old, not tight and old!
Senses, raging, in need of colour
as we behold ourselves, mirror-wise,
the women we always were,
just older, looser, still there.

Ageing Girls

collect fabric, gold-leaf,
phials of silky fat
from unborn calves.
Over the years
turn inside out,
resolving what was hidden,
like a jet roaring
down the runway
of an unvisited country.
The place is dusty,
guards drugged,
unobservant
of each new arrival.
They parade the avenues,
stroll below storks
in high trees,
enjoying quiet nights,
nets of stars.
Prolapses repaired,
faces tightly injected,
they dress to kill
so they can live.
When they strip
by the shore,
nobody cares,
nor if they spend, gamble,
drop twenty years
in a certain light.
A few kleptos prosper

as never before,
then gradually stop,
appeased.
The moneyed
carry on as usual,
the rest too,
who always knew that this
would come. Finally,
the play of moist lipsticks,
flimsies for beneath a skirt
where all, at last,
is private. Time
to ascend
an open gaming table,
to pass floats
with dancers,
gleaming men
who leave them be.
Still beautiful,
vocational,
they present their coins,
their slim gold cards.

Girls of the Nation

They settle in thousands, don't spit or wear purple,
Run their sticks along park railings to frighten the swans.
Plumage is maintained by pensions, small inheritances
From dutiful husbands. A new jacket each winter
Slides smooth over quill-brittle arms.
There are day-trips to Sligo, Kilkenny, Belfast,
A gang flight through the aisles of M & S –
Luxury, prepared dinners, new thermals – and
Midnight-blue balcony bras, just in case.
A bottle or two from each trip builds to a stash
For when the mood takes some of them back: autumn
Trips in better times – Sorrento, the Amalfi Coast,
When they were dazzled by the pink cliffs, unruffled sea,
That train-ride to Rapallo, from where a poet set sail,
Coffined for America. Free of children, at one
With escapee painters, poets, who nuzzled their way
To Mediterranean nests; at one with the unscandaled
Pace – free, inventable on evening promenades
Past white boats, yellow moorings, their fingers entwined
In someone else's. Now it's cafes, Tuesdays with the girls,
Holding their breath as someone else's memory
Falls off the shelf. Secret atheists, they believe in nothing,
Only that final shredding when all they have discovered
Is unlearned again, and flights of meaning
Moult into nothingness. At six, they separate,
Hurry down the moving stairway to a rendezvous,
Not with heaven, but a car-park beside an ordinary lake,
Where even the swans are in a rush.

Breaking the Border

Down the long boulevards,
looking to Mexico from between the palms,
I held my sister's hand, invisibly,
as we prowled the shops
and danced with the dead,
shaking skeletons till their clothes fell off.
Later I dreamed of earthquakes,
the company of an old queen
who nailed himself in his own coffin,
but the dead we danced with that day
put flesh on our sisterhood.
At last on the boulevards,
my blonde sister and I,
at play in animal print, shades,
posing before the mannequins,
dancing with the dead of old Mexico.

Café Terrace at Night, 1888

The waiter at Arles, white-aproned,
Tray in hand before a solitary man.
At other tables, women sit beneath the awning,

Heliotrope yellows above and behind,
On a deck that skims the cobbles.
These sitters are un-posed, indifferent

To the artist painting some distance
Up the street, companions, drawn for
Coffee, absinthe, or conversation.

The invisible is touched on, feet
Toe gently at the floor beneath a chair
Where no-one notices the telltale movement.

To the right, a couple is about to vanish
Down a street where night has fallen
And frugal rooms are lit. They

Have somewhere to go, footsteps intimate
Beneath wavering stars.
This morning I turn to those yellows

On Van Gogh's café terrace,
Atavistic, darkly cottoned, like
The woman with the red shawl,

Head inclined like a bird.

Considering Puccini's Women

"The passion can go and take a running jump at itself,
that's what it can take."

NUALA O'FAOLAIN

See the maestro in retreat! The guide sighs,
waves his hand grandly: medals,
photographs, the 1902 automobile, boats,
women. A place where solitude, she suspects,
was not the essence.

This house resounded with feasting, singing
near a window overlooking the lake.
She regards her companion, considering what seems
a different way. From the first
they too created tempests, almost breaking
in the onslaught.

Now, tourists at Torre del Lago, their eyes
undress the maestro's summer home. They
sandal-shush from room to room,
in shuttered midday;
his piano is revealed, beside it the composition table
where Mimi came to life, and Butterfly broke.

She ponders Puccini's women,
his men, but mostly the women whose article of faith
was a processional of mistaken motive.

Again, the tarnished medals hold her, automobile,
boats, portraits of his women: irritated, she pulls
from her companion's arm, considering a world of
his, his, and more *his.* Beauty, love,
the vaunt of life in time, so clearly at the heart,
now draw themselves around as if to comfort.
Absence and adventure, they taunt.

Summer, Salsomaggiore
for Kate and Dermot

The cousins come again, four years
from the last party in the violet hills.
They quicken at the sight of one another,
rare sightings making moments precious.

Since the last, one party-goer has left,
fought her cancer, talked of new beginnings.
There were none, only continuity,
the hope of drawing down, like the cousins,
another thread from the garment of memory,
childhood's trove of misremembered tales,
chased and polished to fit the need of each.

Around the evening garden, they wander,
mingle beneath a sunset-hammered sky,
freed around the pool.

Later, Cohen's on her mind,
dance me to the end of love, but the couples,
unromantic to the last, are whirling demons
loosed beneath the marquee.
Suddenly, a husband caught off-guard,
his eyes uncertain, as if the scene
has somehow unnerved him.

She wants to leave the cousins' chatter,
the narcissism of camera-flare
at every move and smile, run with him
down past the pool, slip off her satin,
she and he in a madness of leaves,
late, gummy gnats, the hillside moths.

The Sisters of Viareggio

Anna flips into the waves
and in the deck-chair our holiday begins.
I drowse in the busy quiet of shaded women
and gossip, near a solitary Papa,
his crackling newspaper.

Madonnas suckle infants,
call children, scold and cuddle.
A young mother spoon-feeds her twins,
surrounded by beneficience,
smiling companions of dark eye
and hair, straight from Raphael.

Down the beach, our daughter emerges
from a skim of waves; her hair drips
and curls, an un-landed smile
marking her arrival with a surfboard
on the sand. Local boys thud footballs.
She skitters back through the shallows,
ignoring them, her smile confiding nothing,
bright as a shell.

II

Explorer

Forensic as a palaeontologist,
he peers patiently into our hearts,
at weighted layers, slivered imprints
from the time of wolves and deep forest.

Education borne lightly – a backpack
of grim sandwiches, guide books, three pairs
of knitted socks. Loves our language
as much as the bog. His gaze, his ear,
bless the black crumble of both,
though the people keep faith with neither.

His secular attention rises over lakes,
inlets, cloud-ghosted Maamturks; otters
and badgers are a siren-choir
that lures him year on year.

He does not smile easily
unless stirred by authentic local comment,
sometimes forgetting all debate is local,
that those who live the collage, the postcard,
can separate the textures for themselves,
spin worldly yarns in places called 'home'.

His archetypal face you recognise – large-nosed,
unfreckled, deep-eyed – pushing on, at ease
with his search, somehow still peasant,
a potato-eater long ago dispossessed
from some Dutch or Silesian farm,
here, among us, still seeking home.

Les Français sont arrivés,
Die Deutschen auch

Time to roll out the blanket of our best,
weft of wools, rain-whipped streets
of a western town, lattes
and espressos our forebears sipped
before the hay was in and sunset
turned fields to flattened reeds of gold,
visions of the way we never were.

Time to hawk hairy sweaters,
rolls of tweed, sea views,
horses, open skies;
pottery and artisan breads,
butter churned by fairies
when the moon's waxing.

Fish-loving français gobble
all the salmon, the Germans
cannot walk enough beneath
cloud-sailed skies, where limestone
ribs encase the Burren,
and we in our tented streets
of emerald cabbages, fearing stone walls
might fall and fill again
the fields despised by Cromwell.

So, hairy sweaters all the way,
fiddle-me-flagrant on the flagstones,
jig-em-to-hell at dolmens, cliff paths,
wherever life-smudged innocents
are drawn to beauty or
a long note, cast out as if to say
whatever you sing, sing nothing.

Forget the lament in the shape of a road,
how fairies cursed one house
but danced at another. Don't reveal
the changeling self as the knit-wit island
laughs all the way to Dun an Airgid,
just thank the times,
forget the memory of mists and mires,
cloaked crones and weed-winkled
cross-roads, undirected leaves,
the heat of August, penetrative, fruiting,
what filled us once although
we knew not how.

Burren Falcon

Roused, she unpleats her feathers in the wind,
shakes her head, takes a quick shit, unloading
before flight. The sky pours hunting inks of colour:
pupils enlarge, fill the eye's pool. Mountain,
dolmen, ferns, hem the low outcrops where
ascent begins again. She escapes the falconer's arm,
outward though not half far enough,
her senses mewl for mice, chicks, newborn lambs
with sweet eyes and succulent hearts. Erect
with desire, her feathers flatten, she is scattershot
in the sky's skin, blood-charged as she lunges
where limestone encloses the mountain's
lungs. She tears on to a little death, beak
like a hooked needle, finally threading flesh.

The Poulnabrone Dolmen

She scowls at the horizon, opens up
her phone, trails us on the holiday route.

Every comment that day announces
sullen unsurprise. Girl, frog-marched, texting

through the Burren, *all those sad rocks!* she moans.
We inflict on her our Celtic marvels,

the ancient dead within stone chambers, porticos
and grykes. After, a photo shows a cloud-bank,

the capstone, her averted face; the dolmen,
shouldering the sky, squat-haunched

in a wilderness, as much itself in spleen
as she is now. I touch the stone as if to feel

it breathe. Instead I brush against my daughter's
rightful grit as she resists, resists the culture

of the tribe that, today, tells her things
she does not want to know.

Heat

The once-blue ice is turning grey and soft.
Out on the wastes, rumours of skilled hunters,
long plunged beneath ice that tore like skin.
White bears head for the suburbs,
loose-pelted, drawn by the reek of leftovers

to raid trash-cans, rubbish-tips. Every winter,
their daring grows despite varmint rifles,
men who press the rounds in, shoot into
the night, then aim again, their breath
a whisper of ice with each retort.

The bears' earth has lost its touch,
paws and claws no longer feel
stability on the deep ice-plateaux.
The only message is of earth's dementia,
her watery heart fibrillating.

A huge gate swings back, water flows,
no longer rigged in cliffs to the ocean bed.
Melt-brained, the ice slides south, deserting
the animals. Arkless – fox, wolf and bear
forage towards the towns.

An Amnesiac in Dublin

I

I know this city like my hand,
read and re-read a palmist's map
to a forgotten dream.
How reliable is that?
Drawn by the harmless filth,
I return at night. Streets and leaning houses
are displaced. Lighting is Victorian,
throws dusky shafts on girls in bustles,
men with dark suits, tilted hats, jaunty canes.
The Quays tilt as in a Gaudi drawing,
trams roll, the faces within from Renoir's
parties. I throw my lot in with these revellers.

II

The waking dream is different.
As friends, we trip the bridges
that lace the city's bodice north to south,
traverse a Liffey lit by tasselled strobes.
Hamburg-meets-Dublin, unofficial pimps
work the river's walled thighs. Bodies
curl chin to knee in cardboard duvets,
the air around them urinary as the wind
blasts daggers up the estuary.
The Quays still tilt as in Gaudi.

We laugh, we bundle our breasts high and tight,
make spikes in hired wigs, ready to dance jigs
around a Salsa.
              After-hours faces in trams are work-dazed;
taxis dodge O'Connell Street,
              the Battle of the Burger,
                     Little Africa
                            and *Beijing Nua.*
              Amnesiac to the present,
we avert our faces, try to recall older struggles:
Lockout, Rising, the death of Collins;
amnesiac, we remember the war we took no part in
while the infant state's arse was slapped to life,
amnesiac, we quote by heart the rights of those
who scarcely breathed but gradually exhaled
through the 70s, 80s, can call the roll
of those who left, then returned, bringing others.

III

Friends, I know this city like my hand,
drink and dance, fiddle freely
with the coked-up dissolute.
There's fakery at work. I too am fake
in fishnet tights, pretending as I strut
around the voodoo haunts, darkened, oily arches
where women hunker down to piss.
Yet it's hardly time for furry slippers,

34

a bed-jacket. What ill-formed creature
crouches within such braggadocio,
the fuckem and forgetem? Sometimes,
we are no more than succubi
to some other half's unconscious,
tram-rolled, dread,
the Quays still tilting.

The Mess of Our Lives

This summer has two states – rain and non-rain.
Above banked clouds, jets stream west, south.
Night and day the scream of engines.
So low the cloud, helicopters are invisible.
Rooftops are opaque, those blade-sharp lines
against twilight blue, long absent.

Clammy, we dance in pubs near the river,
spill onto footpaths, stagger
along the estuary towards electric dawns.
Sailors move out from the heaving warrens
they have graced for brief days. Our loneliness
mounts. When we tuck up together, it is
not enough, you behind me, your strong fingers,
that curved thumb around my ribs, my mottled
skirt rising, neither of us bothering
to undress. We retreat from wondering
how to pass hours, minutes when we cannot see
roofs, when helicopters disappear
and swallows fly so low they slip
through the hot grilles of cars
discharging from bridges at evening.

Last night, somewhere up there, was full moon.
I tugged the blind and gazed at the river,
sensing sludge. I imagined a ghostly
filly on the water, hooves by-stepping
the mess, perturbed as poetry,
made in all weathers.

I'd say it's a sign.

Of something. Somewhere.

D' fuck? you grumbled as I shook you awake.

D'fuck ya doin?

Within the Secret State

Twenty years ago, it felt
like a secret explosion across despair:

I would have slipped out early between night
and humans. Cycled to the village. Ticking wheels.

Frightened rooks scattered above exhausted pubs
to craw on the aerials, cackle on roofs.

Nobody rose before eight, the only smell
came from unloaded grain at the mill.

Pre-dawn primitive tangling with poky village,
I dumped the bike in the hedgerows,

whipped wet, aroused weeds with my hand,
slipped, ran, crossing stream

to field the undiscovered territory,
my *Australis*, my found South.

This morning, after so long, the call again.
Quickly, the same evaporation of self from house,

no bike, just feet, the need to walk hand in hand
beside a secret, in a time when I thought

that none remained. High-security homes
doze through the dawn, bedrooms blinded,

gates bolted, motion-detectors watchful.
Four-wheelers face out, as if to spring.

I quickly pass by. Away then, up the road
to the spread field where humming barley

catches the last mist and the sun throws
a limb of delight across the world's deep bed.

Rain, That Thief

We thought nothing of wet summers, packed the wellies,
Foxford wool blanket, sandals, flasks and teabags.
Headlands, light-houses, were our goal,
my father's pipe-smoke filling the car sweetly,
blue air within, mauve outside,
                              where clouds were snatched
by wild waves at The Hook, or Carnivan.

West Cork inlets were quieter, crab-filled fingers between hill
and hill. Sea-mists breathed. There was no earth. We drifted,
became wee and hidden through the miraculous fabric of water,
                              happy to be stolen.

Later, in love, rain fell like lavender needles, a fairy boy's
cheek rested on mine, our noses glided, we were invisible
                              and warm by the lake, as rain
speckled the surface between reeds, near the still trout.

Older, I quarrelled with another, words struck the ceiling
above separate hotel beds. Outside, the overflow,
                              singing gullies when we were spent.

Dark clouds break this summer. Again, I am stolen,
still travelling, forget to grieve. This water-land takes me,
misfit mortal, to flowing point.
High above the falls, I have wings.

A Young Fisherman Waits for the Weather to Change

Since we anchored two hookers, *leath bhád**
agus bád mór, together in the harbour,
our luck is gone.

The morning of the wedding,
I glanced uneasily at the sky: *this is folly,*
I whispered, too polite to speak aloud
in the presence of her parents.
All summer the mist, sweeping our island.
Sailing impossible, boats tied,
some smashed by fists of storms,
what some call 'rain god'.

In a new home, we play with gadgets,
each room too white, too defined by what we own.
We fiddle with things. We tease one another.
In the absence of play, roughness,
anger as, yet again, the sky pummels down.
At times, she looks at me queerly.

On the computer, on television, the weatherman
forfeits old charms for the sake of bottled tan,
bleached teeth, the pace of World Wide Weather.
In essence, *nimbo*-this and *strato*-that, all leading
to afternoons of *cumulonimbus,*

* traditional boats once used in the West of Ireland

when we distract ourselves in a swirl
of unchanged linen, pillows that smell of us.

Tonight the sky drops like a heavy lid,
tight on my shoulders, not a star in sight
for wishing on, leaving only
wraiths that squat on our roof.
There is nothing to pray to.

Come, winter! Our haul of haddock,
sardines, the meaty lobster she craves.
Come, winter, long and cold,
with hoar-frost, pelts of northern wind
drying our barrels, silencing the gutter!

I wait for cirrus – a high screen of ice,
crystal haloes above the water, the secret
shoals: sea and sky for once holding distant,
as if in recognition. Then, the boats
recreated in fresh pitch,
umber sails hoisted. The pair of us
at work we know, salt in the creases
around our eyes.

Fairy Rath*

Here lie the faggoted bones of babies –
stillborn, miscarried, or unbaptised,
returned to the fairies who borrow souls.
They do not mean to hold,
long to test themselves in human traces,
imagine the possibility of blood,
the beating logic of a good heart,
dividing cells, pink fingertips,
the casings of a child's nails.

But some fear to pass. Drivers
hurry downhill, graze pot-holes in the rush,
avoid small voices
　　　　at the shelf-edge of hearing.
Walkers scuttle, call dogs to heel.
　　　　Yet I hear no dark whisper,
have sat within view of the rath
on an April Monday,
when the estral celebration is at an end,
near the beech whose roots feed off the wets,
below circling daffodils,
what some believe are rotten.
Bluebells toss in tides, the big field groans
and cracks to life around the rath,
pushing the load of young barley.

* a pre-historic earthen-banked fort

I could be stocked, mocked for the shame
of superstition. I hear what I hear,
know what I know: voices behind birdsong,
ticking wings the underside of leaves,
the quick buzz as they set out,
humming to those who've passed
and go no further. They bear them back
to this safe place, unthieved, borrowed.
Within the circle, all is wholesome:
the sentried rath, soil stitched with bone
fine as porcelain. Old gods lean in close.

Christmas

this tree & the unlit wood
    this wood & the loamy dusk
        an ice-fog enters the lungs

you cough back the wet crystals as you walk
    urge the dog on through the wood
        past the ruined castle

not knowing the why of this search
    but it's Christmas and something
        has driven you out to the silence

where a crepuscular light is at odds
    with the lit houses outside the wood
        so that you feel the parental planet

still home to you the dog the elderly trees
    in their December garment of trust & you
        can trust a hoar that breathes

down on the wood from the high atmosphere
    limitless & touching it carries you
        up and out yet below in near-dark

you whirl at year's end two circling, animal ghosts
    keeping time marking the trees
        skirting the lake dancing

    happy & lightless with the galaxy

Lovers Can Disregard It All

Although it was summer, we took the rain on our tongues,
caught broken cloud, those mis-matched threads
like worn fabric from a beggar's back.
What remained was to lie down
in the uncut meadow, so wet we were naked,
with an extra-thin skin, the flags and vetches
mirrored in our eyes.

The Ark Builders

Murders as usual for the time of year,
although no sun to speak of. Weekends are heated.
We survive in the deluge, drink and dance, spending
fast as we pump it up, *pump-pump, pump-pump.*
Black cars nose through the suburbs,
slash torrential roads, four heads or five,
close-cut, pit-vipers, strong, stronger, strongest,
muscle-twisting, chest-beating.
Every house an ark where the kids
shoot up, two by two,
share glittering spoons.
Noah and Mrs. Noah are long gone.
Rain continues to fall

III

Santiago De Compostela

Movement, silence, live here. Hold your breath,
await the many parts of yourself.
Walkers clatter into the city, exhausted,
tearful. They laugh and sing on the final trek
to the Cathedral. Studs on their boots
clash with stone as they climb steps,
then enter the vaulted space.
       Having arrived, the group scatters.
       Some for confession, others seek James,
embrace the statue, weep openly.
Prayer is public. They are not shy
to cross themselves and kneel.

Some rod in your soul runs resistant,
though there are instances you could unravel
for a priest, testing the deep ear,
adding to his store of secrets.
Instead, you wander between pillars during Mass,
draw down ropes of miraculous legend.
You see yourself swim with the man who fell
overboard, but made his way ashore, draped
in a cloak of cockle-shells; you travel
an imagined middle-east, noting down,
companionably, the saintly ways, the by-roads,
and who he spoke to. You accompany his body,
on the long route to the western ocean.

Growing into Irish Through Galicia

One morning you wander the streets of Santiago.
    Too late to turn or hide,
way-laid by sound, the raid
    On your closed ear more than a whisper
of music flooding the *rua*,
    a golden furl from the Hebrides to Africa,
caught in a summer-fired sieve.

Young men perform with *Uilleann* pipes,
bodhrán, barrelling rhythms, wrist-flex, shoulder-roll,
    the music of ancient fields and isolation,
where rain drenches memory.
    In the shops, you pit your native tongue
against theirs, meet a Galician poet
    with red hair to her hips and the nose
of an ancient queen, full of her knowledge.

Late learner, half-blind, tone-deaf.
    Not your fault of course,
blame background, the Border, the bashful
    silk of English,
one language hushed by the rhythms of the other,
    until this rush to the senses.

By the time you pack for home, your tongue
    has lost its proud edge of English silk,
You lug new words like a swarm of bees,
    (the sting of honour, a carrier at last).
No longer backed up against the tide,

the shell of your hearing opens,
old words roll like sand in mussel-flesh,
   grit to a pearl. And you are readied
To grow hair to the hips, though your nose
   is small and you have only
questions. This morning in Galicia, you are free
   and know it, cross the Praza da Paz in a chant,
hear answering chords, your tongue unsprung:
   it fills your mouth like hymns
rising to a vaulted roof, and filled,
   you expand, singing out hellos,
Ireland to Galicia and back again:
   Fáilte, fáilte, fáilte!

Only on the Edge

Some call them tufts: doughty phyla
on a cliff-ledge, undiminished
by the brawn of land.

Flos Hibernicus, Armorica Purpuria,
Foliae Galiciae, Vimen Longum
Albaea, Cornish Spindle.

Flos Hibernicus quivers,
its yellow heart polleny. *Foliae*
Galiciae unfolds and twitches,
braced against rod-iron grass,
beside *Vimen Longum Albae.*

Cornish Spindle crawls from Albion's
fingernails, the heavy fruit of English
seeds a rocky overhang.

They milk light clean, nestle
on gull ledges when the sun's gone
and unglamorous night tends to word-hoards,
cousinly grammars further up or down
the Continent. They and their like
survive on the cliffs, so far down
the ramblers hardly see.

Earnest, they sketch menhirs,
note in plainest language the crone-
snouted headlands, hoping to unearth
coin, casket, spearhead.
They forget to press an ear
to the lip of the land where language
still flowers, seeking pagan ears
and a modern mouth.

Equatorial

Forty years ago, gaping at bare-breasted
women, I sat on the sofa with buttered
toast dipped in egg, as Africa was revealed

in black-and-white. Animals held me, their eyes
wilder than those of the dogs and cats I pulled
and teased. Those rhythmic crowds returned tonight,

half-robed in yellow, sticks and spears raised
as the man from the BBC leads armchair travellers
through the Congo, Gabon, on to Kenya.

The uninhibited media noses
along Earth's rounded belly, its mottled gold,
its mud, child slaves. Clouds seethe, throw shadows

on clustered forests; the speaker points
to infested rivers, Eboli, AIDS,
the rainbow of misery, and treacherous armies.

On the programme, a man has walked twenty
kilometres, four stone of wood biting
his shoulders, a girl in half a dress has never been

beyond the camp; the circumcisor makes
a hundred daily cuts on waiting boys –
the catalogue of what we hear when things

go wrong. But it's Sunday night, and surely
there's more to Africa, some unfilmed truth –
casual, sweet. Now north-drawn dark edges in,

September presses down its woolly weight.
Already, a fire is lit, kettle boils,
sends clouds in puffs – shadows on the week ahead.

The Sea Knows
for Luz Mar Gonzales Arias

You dive into Pacific surf
on a winter beach, miss the whales
passing at night on their way to mate,
spend days in the moiling waves,
your bikini ripped with the force.
       At night, you cannot sleep.
The heat and humid air a film too familiar
with your flesh.

       *

You snorkel far from the shore,
drift on the surface
beyond Julius Rock, adjusting,
a first-timer, weak in that current.
Yet you need to see what lies below:
gigolo sharks, eye-catching playboys,
old-girl curmudgeons too,
their stripes brown, orange,
all cream-flounced tail as they grumble past.
       And still at night, you do not
sleep. Heat and humid air offer themselves
as second skins.

       *

Then, mackerel-fishing
beyond tide-spurred shallows,
casting line, the quiet tick-tick,
effortless water-slobber
of an ancient boat, outboard
silent as you wait, the wind
roughing skin as you bend and peer,
hoping for shoals, hoping
to catch the mackerel – pull,
fling the full slittering stream
of your sex just one last time,
before returning her quick and quiet
to her own place. You start
the motor, turn for shore.

      That night, you dream
of the galactic sperm of whales,
of spumous release within the waves.
A sky of mackerel races in your blood.

A Need for Devil's Pokers

His considerate stealth means
you never notice he's left the bed,
dressed, shut the door. This morning

you stir to the quick crunch

of the car on gravel as he sets off,
city-bound. You imagine
his flapping morning coat,

the stormed city as he quickens

through doors, face set to listen
at some round table beneath prismic glass,
king among knights. Invisible

his crown, they sense the un-stoned sword

which stays him. He has no thought
of shapes beyond the infinite circle,
allows all comers. Architect,

financier, spread plans, faces unreadable;

men with chests like jutting robins,
rogue jousting chevaliers who long
to knock him flat.

And you? At home thinking,

as you grind your coffee,
slice that brown soda,
take salmon from the freezer:

o still-young king, beware the Lancelots,

false rhetoric, easy theft in daily speech.
Later, when car wheels crunch and
he slams the door on the day,

you read one another's faces,

two estranged animals,
trading secrets wordlessly.
The skin on the salmon

bubbles gently beneath the grill,

you've burnt your finger
yet again, and suck the blister.
You live for better weather,

the end of storms.

Seven Monaco Haiku

1.

Though my basket fills,
I empty to less and less,
light as a petal.

2.

From the hills they come,
old people to old markets.
Morning's yield of chat.

3.

Catalpa and palms
downhill to the Casino,
ducks in the fountain.

4.

In this autumn light,
heart-swell, a gentle shoreline,
and bougainvillea.

5.

The high labyrinth,
your shutters hung with bright flowers,
graceful pollen-fall.

6.

Castle in the air,
ancient rock, long fingered streets:
I stand quiet in the sun.

7.

I watch from this point
remembering fishermen.
Where are the mermaids?

Blush Season

1.

The tree in April.
Pink feathers settle at night.
By day, birds in flight.

2.

I forget to prune,
Yet yearly, clusters open,
a tree is waiting.

3.

Soft and yet more dense,
if quantity means armfuls,
I embrace this pink.

4.

Blooms for my birthday,
Soft avalanche, cherry drifts.
Another year passing.

Taking the Measure
for Martin Nugent

Thirty years ago, I held your hand, across tables,
in pubs. We walked hissing night streets
in search of *cinema verité*, Woody Allen,
Bertolucci, lingered late for the sake
of threading fingers as you drove one-handedly
home again. I laughed at your jokes. We agreed
that Don McClean had talent, the North
was a mess, the IRA all wrong, but even so
the Brits should go. Taking our measure,
finding it roughly equal, we spread casual words
on music, politics, a few jokes and the message
sent by curling palm to palm.

Last night on our country road you
took my hand beneath a golden moon
that bowled across threshed fields.
We walked. We talked. Household politics.
Gardening dilemmas. A mid-term trip
to Kerry. As before, you increased your grip,
as if afraid that I would slip. But
you got the girl. You got her
when we joined evening queues
for communal hand-to-hand-secrets,
intent on warmth, lightness,
the end of the treasure hunt.

Garage Events

Where you hid the letters
beneath the gas cylinder,
where once you both restored
a desk, rushing to the blonde wood
panels, the green leather surface
a lake lean with light
from the evening sun,
forgiving as you swam together
in the ease of doing.
Where you also found a rat
in a potato-barrel, mistaking it
for a large mouse,
your fingers hooked gently
beneath the heart-bobbing belly.
You lifted it free, noting
the long, ringed tail,
those unblinking, brown eyes.
Small rat, small rat, surprised –
shocked – did not bite, but hung
there, a minky curve in the O
of thumb and finger.
You lowered it to the wood pile.
It paused, then slipped silently
within catacombs of dried birch,
poplar, safe in the dark.

Letting Down His Hair

Free now to wander his lake, his ground,
to pick through the hills, watch the walls,
see the pictures, light the fire, drink
the last of his whiskey, she crosses her legs
and sees herself, below whatever is above.
She imagines a vessel at anchor,
him dropping the rope of his death-grown hair
through the thick underwater of sleep,
hears his voice though his face fragments
no matter how hard she tries to recreate it.
A nostril here, the curve of a lip there,
one watchful eye. She senses his touch
when she turns in the bed,
but waking does not please her.

After

There are no instructions.
There is no correct way of finishing.

Here are the hats, the ties,
suits he wore. See here, the shoes,
rows of them gleaming
when the wardrobe is open
and the sun dances down
the field to the east.

No one tidies here. No one removes.
The poor will not benefit.
Even the human odour of clothes
fades. No mystery to this.
Time does the work.

Dead People's Clothes

Father's blue silk socks.
mother-in-law's scarf.
Grandmother's purse,
aunty's white plastic beads.
So we wear history,
hold onto vacated things
that they once lived in,
historians to the end.

We imagine them here,
as buildings, sometimes too tall,
too oppressive, as so often in life,
no matter the antique charm,
or how we grew in those high rooms,
becoming what we are now:
hooked. Carrying it along
with every step: father's silk socks;
mother-in-law's scarf, those old,
dead people's clothes.
The smell of inheritance
lingers in our nostrils.

Random Questions

You can look things up in a dead person
like in a dictionary
JOHN BERGER

When you get there what's it like?
Could you feel your legs after the trip?
Did anybody greet you? Are you stuck with people
you never really liked, or the few you gave a damn about?
Have I time to visit Argentina, ride horses in the pampas?
Is the Tango all it's cracked up to be?

Now that I'm fifty, should I go to Confession
about the one sin I want rid of? Is there a time
to officially say 'sorry', or is that superstition
of the most primitive kind? Have I time enough to live a dream,
by day and not by night? How'll I handle being alone?
Are Dinners for One the thing over there, or is the banqueting hall
like Hogwarts refectory, floating candles, platters of iced-cake and all?
What about sex and wine? Lots of both, I assume,
just as I like them – room temperature and leisurely,
the menopause an earthly lie about hot-faced
psycho-women – long forgotten?

PS: If replying, no funny apparitions while I'm working,
or banshee wailing in the night. An insight will do the trick,
an ordinary paranormal moment of understanding
when I'm browsing in some shop. Or else silence, you hovering
behind my shoulder, not even whispering as I paint contentedly,
in white dungarees, without make-up or eyelashes,
a bowl of cool Victoria plums, dark grapes, my young love
reclining in his finery of skin…

Scenes from Pre-Life

The ship of the unborn drifts through the cosmos,
docking as required, webbed sails
folding to masts of bone.

En route, each child has playthings –
the only stars, they learn, are the shivering lights
from fore, aft; drums, needles, pieces of metal
that gleam below the galactic suns.

A millennium ago, there's Einstein, fumbling
with the abacus, *m... m... m...* he repeats,
an unrelenting counter of small universes
at his fingertips, irritating to some,
who consider him a dunderhead.
On the upper deck, future singers discover harmony
from observing the spheres; Bono is in thrall to Gigli,
but the light is excessive, he complains,
covering his eyes with the palms of his hands.
Dutch glass-grinders regard him with interest
from sand-boxes, still uncertain of the substance
that sifts through their fingers. Da Vinci rips at the wings
of dead birds, *just to see, just to see,* he mumbles.

Sibelius – forced to wait it out while Mendelsohn,
Beethoven, get shore leave, dashing off concertos
like post-cards to the world –
has nightmares of a country squeezed
within the locked pelvis of Russia, Sweden.

He is not alone, forced to watch, sailing on,
awaiting the call. Coming, it catches them cruelly,
often ripped from sleep: like walking the plank,
then told to find consolation in a blindfold
of amnesia, the beeswax ear-stops of birth,
flailing yet contained in the ever-ness of Arrival.

Now, oddly, all are strangers and life on earth
a series of re-introductions, finally testing
those precocious preparations for what most
have vaguely known: eventual return,
a terrible promise, and revenge.

The Bread-Maker Speaks
after Brendan Kennelly

It is true that you comfort me
As I slit your flesh
When kneading is done,

Marking a cross
To create four quarters.
I am not brutal,

Your crushed kernels,
Have long awaited
The flow from jug to bowl,

Moisture not known since before
You were beheaded
In an August field.

Through milk, you remember rain,
What made you grow.
And I remember another kitchen,

The smell when soda
Was spooned, a pinch of salt,
Melted butter. Each time

My fingers glide
Beneath your thinly-floured
Mound, I learn again how days

And dreams fatten in warmth,
Wetness, barely dusted by
What contains them:

Routine acts, healing
In work, pleasure
In slit and cut.

From the fingers out,
I make shapes.
The oven's belly groans.

Star Reading for a Young Poet

The full head of her blazes
in the light, words not pouring
but on fire. Even the sun
seems dim. Unnamed stars orbit,
spit flame around her shoulders,
allow the poem within, written
and unwritten, coolness
and dispassion before her mouth
opens and all that was molten
on her tongue has the form
of her future.

Misirlou*

How it is, how it has to be.
You, your daughter and Dick Dale
roaring up the road away from the village,
cackling at the rush of asphalt beneath the red hood.
Then the silence, almost, as you listen:
Jungle Boogie, the tin-can bass of *Bullwinkle*
and *Let's Stay Together*, those wilderness men
who slink near the blaze of women's lives,
arriving in hers, departing from yours.

Although you drive to the horizons,
fist gearing up, foot slamming clutch,
easing rapidly to pull beyond the limits,
she's going one way, you the other,
but that's okay, chick and hen
nodding to the rhythm, shoulders twitching
to the vram of *Misirlou*,
and you know who hasn't lived like this:

glossing over the way of things female,
invention in your every cell,
you create the long drive, then rear
into the sleek back of the speed-reddened,
so perfectly formed it stings the eyes to look.
(Could be the best men's art is automobilic).
How you burn the oil and shift that clutch
on the way to god-knows-where!

As you drive, remember
to unlearn the girlie smile,
to seal teeth and tongue behind
the lips' firm purse, remember to stare ahead,
not to flutter lashes; become Isadora
without the scarf
and broken neck, reckless yet knowing,
innocent yet intentional,
you and the girl you're trying to instruct
in subtleties of century-living,
how to span it like a bridge,
to hang loose or rear up from subterranea,
a tectonic presence between the generations,
how to write it before others write it for you.
Windows down, hair flying,
not a thought in your head
but the savage flow of what falls away,
slipping, sliding, aerodynamic as the wind across the top
of a metallic, rearing animal on wheels.
How it is, how it has to be, oh *misirlou*,
misirlou, to the limits and more, now...

* Opening track from Quentin Tarantino's movie *Pulp Fiction.*

Pentacle

i.m. John O'Donohue

Some sharp, pentacled star
pricked you with its random spark,
then cut the thread as you slept.

I think of a lake
seen from a car, Irish-Aegean,
wind-wimpled, a heron in flight.

Wheels turned as we bucked
the thin wilderness roads. Poems quickened.
Shared quicksilver: a sexual shiver

of words, jokes, imaginings for old age,
the ground beneath us firm,
mountains with tunnels to the underworld.

Now, feet have no purchase on road
or mountain, surfaces yield
like tweed collage, its folkish weft

deceiving. The rain-bright stones
no longer wink. Surfaces are sinkholes.
So you are spared old age, skeleton

strong, flesh deeply attached
to bone – out of reach,
out of conversation.

The Bee-Keeper's Son

1. The Women with Lit Lamps

You could not have planned it better,
reach this place to see him borne down
at the pace of final moments,
where the road forks.
Flames flicker in gathering gloom,
women in a beauty of ritual,
with flowers, candles.
The bundling storm
draws thick ropes of cloud,
hurries over the mountain,
a great cloak that hurls itself
beneath sun and rain as the hearse passes,
the whole brown mountain
a whirling fabric as he moves
beyond the limestone fields.

The journey to the church is slow,
and slower crowding.
A priest comforts, a young singer breaks, weeps.
In the vast crowd, that stillness he loved,
in the vast crowd, wildness behind silence,
in the vast crowd, lovers of many kinds
will lament tomorrow.

2. WRITING THE SILENCE

Man of your tribe,
because you described
how you lay across a dolmen in all weathers,
I wrote about rain that trickles down the body
to the fork where legs begin;

because you spoke of mists in your home place
breaking to filled buckets of light,
a feral man crossed my field one winter morning,
hair streaming, good news on his lips.

We entered beauty where you saw it,
embraced the unfinished paradise,
imagining *Eros* when you took each word,
testing it like stone, found the patient angle,
then smacked home when you sensed the fit.

You found flame-keepers,
stone-turners, fleshly men and women:
native of this planet yet estranged.
Man of our tribe, we will not forget
to lie across a dolmen,
run through a misted field at dawn,
empty the bottle, tousle the bed,
write the silence.

3. Swarm in Ballyvaughan*

That summer, being pursued,
the bee-keeper's son grew uneasy.
Bewildered, he stripped by the lake,
ankles breaking the gold skin on water's edge,
a thick sweetness on his lips
when he submerged.

Nor was he alone in the car, after.
Secreted, clinging to the folds of his shirt,
the bees droned constantly, like Nepalese
monks meditating the day and the future.
In sleep, he dreamed of singing emissaries.

Thanatus, they sang, *Thanatus,* they hummed,
so that he caught the three-beat tempo,
played to his heart as on a tuning fork.
My love, he cried, *where is my love?*
Seeking, he brought her to another land,
where he dreamed only her.

But the bees moved as an entity,
urgent with desire for the bee-keeper's son.
An unlatched window, a warm, unguarded night,

* Ballyvaughan: in Irish, Baile Uí Bheacháin, or the Town of the Bee-
keeper.

they gently separated the lovers,
and dressed him in their wings,
made an effigy – a giant bee
in the form of a sleeping man.

4. THE ARK OF BEES

They have carried him here,
high on the water. He is with the animals,

birds he loved, gleam-eyed, ruffle-dashed,
a place for claw and talon, where wolf sleeps with dog.

Sleeping still, he has not
come to his senses, where all at last

is pure synthesis. When he awakens
and sheds the cloak of bees,

the ark continues to drift
slowly across the lost kingdom.

He moves with Noah, with Sabra, his wife,
cleaning stalls of manure, filling feed bins,

drawing water from the deluge without.
Here, everything flows as one.

He sees music in colour, tastes every note
on his tongue, loves the male in women,

the female in men, undivided by the earthly.
His eyes feel with the precision of skin,

skin thrills hungrily to the sight of exotic fruits,
the bulging hold. On waking, he recalls

the final goodbyes, how the people came
to wave him off before letting go.

On waking, he knows what it means
to be finished, Byzantine, beyond ordinary art.

Here, fecundity beyond imagining.
Father to many, his species are diverse,

not alone human. The art of his life
already bears children.

5. Restoration

To this ark, the city's boys have been gathered up,
Wounded or dead, drawn at last to the father
They have never known, their bruises healed,
Cuts stanched, teeth replaced, broken brains restored.

In this ark, three hundred years equals one earthly day.
The necessary span of restoration. They lie
In downy beds in the depths of the hold, fed morsels
That nourish, sip oatey beers to seal off the pounding blood-

Lust. In this ark, they are taught to forget survival.
Such skills are not required. Women tend, turn them,
Surgical and precise, who cannot be desired
In an earthly way, being betrothed to the bee-god.

The boys see visions of insects' wings, hear the voice
They never knew before. Finally, they awaken
After three hundred years, stirred and erect. Enormous
Father of all fathers, an oak tree in his hand, bids them

Rise from their cots. When they falter, finding their feet,
He guides patiently, proud of his diligent mansions.
On his head, a crown of purple hyacinths, on his shoulders
A cape of bees, shifting, humming as he moves. Occasionally,

He takes to his finger a sacrificial bee, one for each boy,
Lays it on the breastbone. The sting is deft, quick,
Pierces the soul so that each boy cries out,
And the creature dies.

That, says the bee-god, *was Purgatory. Now live.*
After, the young men explore mansions once denied them.
Craftsmen abound – carpenters demonstrate
The rudiments of things that hold together: butt, dowel,

Mitre, tools for imagining the world – hammer, claw, mallet,
Chisel, plane, knife and drill. All for making, nothing destroyed.
In this ark, they feel the barrel chest of the bee-god
As he leans in when they lift the first tool. *This is how it works,*

He hums gently, *how I brought the world into being.*
Beneath their fingers, shapes come to life,
Awkward until they return and look again, use the tool,
Discovering how craft repeated gives way to art.

Each three century span, they quicken, at peace
With sounds from within the ark: plane, chisel, blade,
At peace with what's beyond: creaking ropes, the mast
Drying in the sun, a gentle slop of water as the hull cuts on,

On, always west, following the sun. At night
Before sleep, each boy takes a bee in his palm on trust:
A gesture, a touching, creature to creature.

Lines to an Ancestor before An Operation

Stay near. Hold fast
to the thin string of my spirit.
Do not pause for the river pilot,
hide me from his searchlight.

I am not ready to cross, to dock
in the shallows of the other shore.
If my spirit flies farther, bind the string
tightly. I am not yet prepared,

even if curiosity, premature longing,
cause me to rise beyond safe limits.
Watch as I sleep, stay the surgeon's hands
as he raises this quiet part of me

like a new-slung ceiling
in the sagging rafters of my pelvis.
No more nor less than the rest of me,
let me inhabit womb, kidney,

jolting heart, restless brain, small nose,
bright eyes, long fingers, worn,
curling toes, the blunts of my teeth
within whitened crowns, all of me,

what's left, for living in without
the burden of reflection.
Stay close now. Bind an adventurous spirit
to a home that sweetens with every month.

Let me be a kite during this sleep,
flown free, bound despite anaesthetic
to the span of your palm,
unbreakable as the light fails.

Biographical Note

MARY O'DONNELL was born in Monaghan, educated at St. Louis Convent Monaghan and later at St. Patrick's College Maynooth. She holds a BA in German and Philosophy, has studied German to MA level and received a first class honours Higher Diploma in Education at Maynooth.

During the last twenty-eight years her career has reflected various interests. She has been a teacher of English, German and Drama; she worked with the development agency Concern; she has been a translator and worked in journalism as *The Sunday Tribune*'s Drama Critic for three years, following on which she freelanced for a further three years.

She presented and scripted three series of poetry programmes for the national broadcaster RTE Radio. She has a particular interest in poetry in translation and during 2005 and 2006 researched, scripted and presented the RTE Radio programme 'Crossing the Lines', a series which focused on European poetry and included readings from the Czech Republic, Poland, Romania, Hungary, Greece, France, Germany, Spain, Norway and Finland. Today, she teaches creative writing with various groups and for four summers worked on the faculty of the University of Iowa's summer writing program at Trinity College Dublin. She is currently a poetry mentor with Carlow University Pittsburgh Pennsylvania. She has published five previous poetry collections, including the 2007 volume *The Place of Miracles* (New Island, Dublin), as well as three novels and two collections of short fiction.

In December 2001 she was elected to the membership of Aosdána, administered by the Irish Arts Council (An Chomhairle Ealaine), which honours artists engaged in literature, music and the visual arts who have made an outstanding contribution to the arts in Ireland. She is a member of the Irish Writers' Union and has served for three years as an external representative for arts and culture on the Governing Authority of the National University of Ireland, Maynooth. Mary O'Donnell now lives near Straffan, County Kildare.

www.maryodonnell.com

Recent titles in Arc Publications'
POETRY FROM THE UK / IRELAND,
include:

LIZ ALMOND
The Shut Drawer
Yelp!

JONATHAN ASSER
Outside The All Stars

DONALD ATKINSON
In Waterlight: Poems New, Selected & Revised

JOANNA BOULTER
Twenty Four Preludes & Fugues
on Dmitri Shostakovich

THOMAS A CLARK
The Path to the Sea

TONY CURTIS
What Darkness Covers
The Well in the Rain

JULIA DARLING
Sudden Collapses in Public Places
Apology for Absence

CHRIS EMERY
Dr. Mephisto
Radio Nostalgia

KATHERINE GALLAGHER
Circus-Apprentice

CHRISSIE GITTINS
Armature

MICHAEL HASLAM
The Music Laid Her Songs in Language
A Sinner Saved by Grace

MICHAEL HULSE
The Secret History